The Life and Work of Henry Moore

Sean Connolly

www.heinemann.co.uk/library
Visit our website to find out more information about **Heinemann Library** books.

To order:
- Phone 44 (0) 1865 888066
- Send a fax to 44 (0) 1865 314091
- Visit the Heinemann Bookshop at www.heinemann.co.uk/library to browse our catalogue and order online.

First published in Great Britain by Heinemann Library, Halley Court, Jordan Hill, Oxford OX2 8EJ, part of Harcourt Education.
Heinemann is a registered trademark of Harcourt Education Ltd.

Second edition first published in paperback in 2007

Editorial: Clare Lewis
Design: Jo Hinton-Malivoire and Q2A Creative

rinting

British Library Cataloguing in Publication Data
Conolly, Sean
The Life and Work of: Henry Moore - 2nd edition
730.9'2
A full catalogue record for this book is available from the British Library.

Acknowledgements
The publishers would like to thank the following for permission to reproduce photographs:
Page 4, Portrait Studio, 1960. Page 5, Henry Moore *Three Forms: Vertebrae*. Page 6, Henry Moore aged 11. Page 7, Castleford Grammar School's Roll of Honour. Page 8, Henry Moore convalescing at Castleford Grammar School, 1918. Page 9, Henry Moore *Small animal head 1921*. Page 10, Corner of Studio Adie Road 1928. Page 11, Henry Moore *Reclining figure 1929*. Page 12, Henry Moore with *West wind* 1928. Page 13, North wall of Headquarters of London Underground. Page 14, Corner of studio at 11a Parkhill Road Hampstead 1936. Page 15, Henry Moore *Reclining figure 1936*. Page 17, Henry Moore *Two forms 1934*. Page 18, Lee Miller, Henry Moore in Holborn Underground, London 1943. Page 19, Henry Moore *Pink and green sleepers 1941*. Page 20, Lee Miller Archives, Henry Moore with Severini in Venice for the Biennale 1948. Page 21, Henry Moore *Madonna and child*. Page 22, Henry Moore carving *UNESCO Reclining figure 1957-58*. Page 23 Henry Moore *Draped Reclining figure 1952-53*. Page 24, Henry Moore in Top Studio 1954. Page 25, Henry Moore *Double oval*. Page 26, Henry Moore working in new maquette studio 1978. Page 27, Henry Moore *Sheep piece 1962-63*. Page 28, The Independent. Page 29, Henry Moore *Large figure in a shelter 1952-53*. Page 16, Robert Harding Picture Library.

Cover photograph: *Family group* - artist collection -Moore, Henry Spencer, reproduced by permssion of Phillips the international fine art auctioneers UK, c. Bonhams, London, UK / Bridgeman Art Library.

The publishers would like to thank Nancy Harris for her assistance in the preparation of this book.

Every effort has been made to contact copyright holders of any material reproduced in this book. Any omissions will be rectified in subsequent printings if notice is given to the publishers.

The paper used to print this book comes from sustainable resources.

Some words in the book are bold, **like this**. You can find out what they mean by looking in the Glossary.

Contents

Who was Henry Moore?

Henry Moore was a very important artist. He made huge **sculptures** out of stone, wood, and a metal called **bronze**. He also made many drawings.

People from around the world asked Henry to make sculptures for them. This sculpture, made in 1978, stands in Dallas, USA.

Early years

Henry Moore was born on 30 July 1898 in Castleford, England. His father was a **miner**. When Henry was 12 years old he went to Castleford Grammar School.

Henry was already good at art. When he was 16 years old his teachers asked him to **carve** this **roll of honour** for the school.

London and Paris

Henry fought in the **First World War** for two years. In 1921 he began studying at the Royal College of Art in London. Two years later he visited Paris in France.

Henry saw many types of art in London and Paris. Henry made this **sculpture** of a small animal head in London in 1921.

Settling in

In 1925 Henry became a teacher at the Royal College of Art in London. He was also busy making his own **sculptures**. In 1928 he had an **exhibition** in London.

Henry **carved** his sculptures out of stone.
He liked to show people lying on their side.
He made many more sculptures like this one.

The public eye

Henry became more famous. When he was 31 he had his first **commission**. It was a huge **sculpture** for the London Underground.

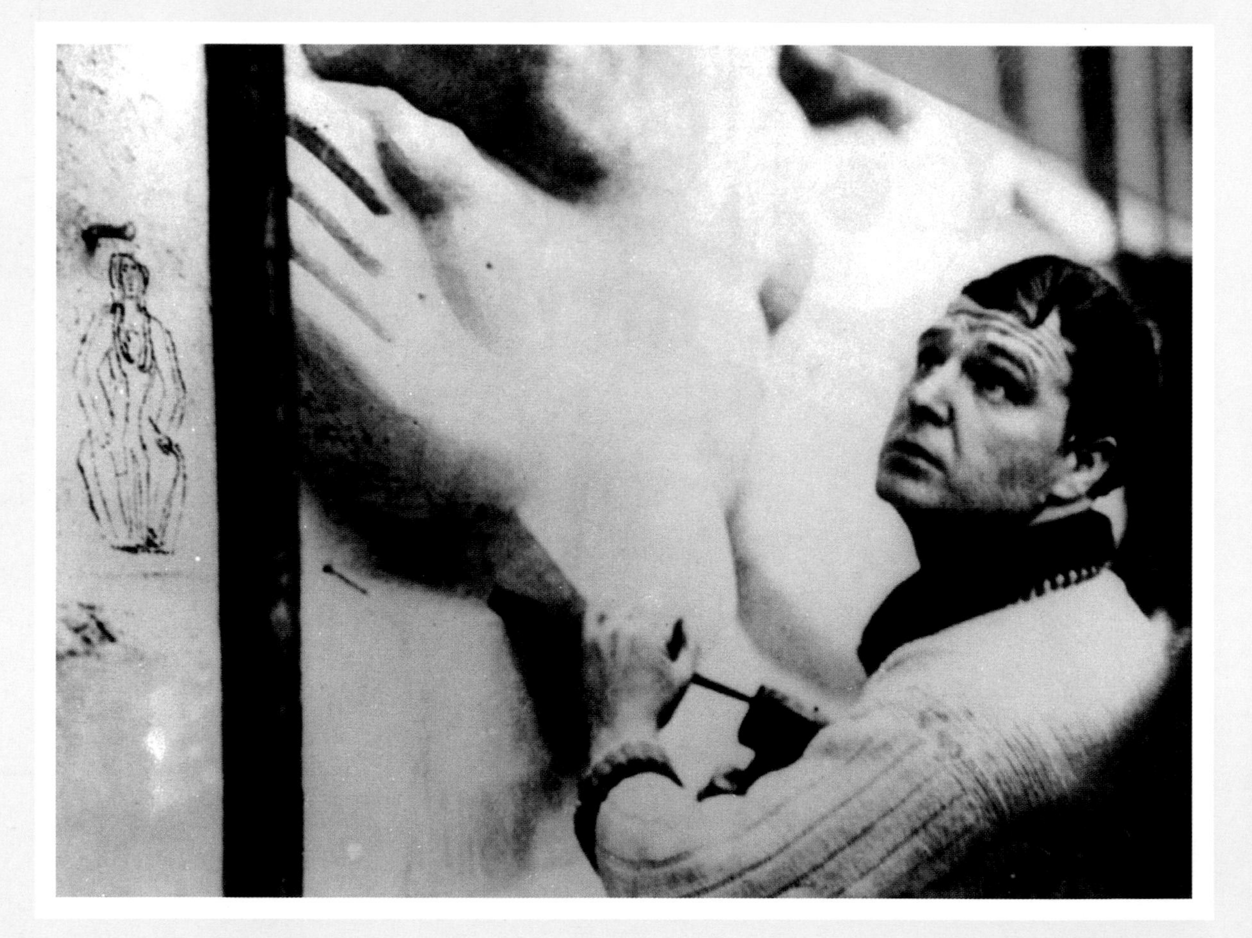

The title of this sculpture was *The North Wind*. It shows Henry's interest in stone, fire, water, and wind.

The modern world

In the 1930s Henry became interested in **abstract art**. His **sculptures** began to look less like human beings and more like simple, rounded shapes.

Henry collected pebbles, stones, and shells to see how nature creates shapes. This statue shows Henry's interest in smooth, curved surfaces.

Getting known

More and more people saw the beauty in Henry's large **sculptures**. They were **exhibited** in Europe and the USA. This is a picture of the Museum of Modern Art in New York, USA.

Henry sold this sculpture to the Museum of Modern Art in New York, USA. It shows how his sculptures were only partly **abstract**. Here you can still see human shapes.

War artist

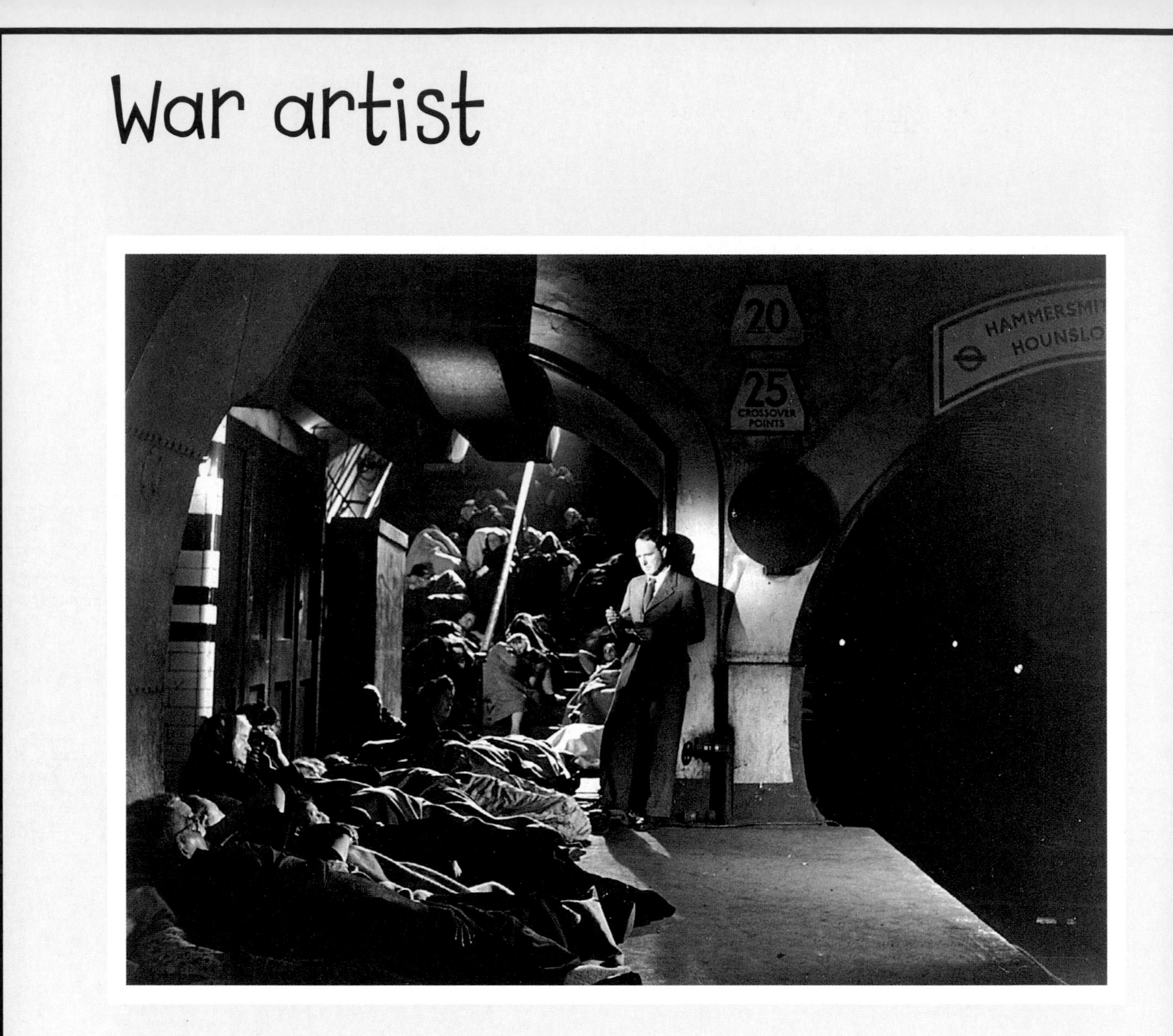

The **Second World War** began in 1939. Two years later Henry became an official war artist. He drew the daily life of people in London during the war.

These drawings are some of Henry's most powerful works. This one shows people trying to sleep while bombs explode outside.

Travelling the world

After the war Henry travelled to many places. He got many awards and prizes for his **sculptures**. This picture shows Henry and a friend in Venice, Italy.

Henry's prizes did not change his way of thinking. He made this **tender** sculpture of Mary and Jesus for a church in Northampton.

Time for a change

In the 1950s Henry tried new ways of working. Until then he **carved** directly from stone. Now he made many **sculptures** from **bronze** and wood.

Henry could make even bigger, smoother sculptures out of bronze. This sculpture of a woman is in front of a building in London.

New ideas

Henry also looked for new ideas. In the 1960s he began putting one shape inside another one. Many of these combined shapes created **hollow sculptures**.

Henry wanted people to look at his large sculptures from all sides. These two oval shapes seem alike at first. They only look different when you walk around them.

The sculptor's studio

Henry moved to Perry Green in Hertfordshire when London was bombed during the war. He was very happy there.

There were sheep in the field outside Henry's **studio**. In the 1970s Henry made many **sketches** of the sheep. He made this **sculpture** to go in the field.

An active life ends

Mourning Henry Moore yesterday: Jeremy Thorpe; Lord Snowdon and Sir Hugh Casson; Moore's daughter Mary Danowski and her children; Michael Foot and his wife, Jill Craigie.

Friends pay tribute to Moore

FELLOW ARTISTS and friends of the sculptor Henry Moore paid their last respects at a memorial service in Westminster Abbey yesterday. Many of his surviving contemporaries including his widow, Irina, whom he married in 1929, were too frail to attend.

Sir Stephen Spender, the poet, told the congregation that Moore, who died in August, aged 88, was the seventh son of a Yorkshire miner who never considered anyone either socially superior or inferior to himself.

Sir Stephen, one of the last surviving members of Moore's avant-garde Hampstead artistic circle in the Thirties, delivered the address in a brisk, husky whisper. He remembered Moore's studio as a focal point for artists, including Ben Nicholson, the painter, and Barbara Hepworth, the sculptress.

He said that despite Moore's admiration for the abstract artists around him, "he told me he could never make an artefact which referred to nothing but itself".

Moore had confided to him: "Try as I might, my work always ended up looking like something, probably a reclining figure."

Sir Stephen quoted Sir Herbert Read, the poet and art critic, and a champion of Moore in the Thirties, saying that in his opinion the sculptor would have been the best possible ambassador from this planet to another.

Sir Stephen said: "He was an artist of great ingenuity and a man of great humanity." Moore had never forgotten the simplicity of his upbringing.

Dame Peggy Ashcroft, the actress, read the first lesson, not from the Bible but from the Apocrypha, the second book of Esdras. It concluded: "He who made all things, and searcheth out hidden things in hidden places, surely he knoweth your imagination, and what ye think in your hearts." The text was suggested to the Moore family by Westminster Abbey, because its words were so appropriate.

The second lesson, read by the Duke of Gloucester, was from Revelations, in the King James version, chosen because it is the one familiar to Moore's generation.

The congregation included the Prime Minister; Michael Foot, the former Labour leader; Sir Hugh Casson, the architect and painter; Sir Roy Strong, director of the Victoria and Albert Museum; Jeremy Thorpe, the former Liberal leader; John Profumo, the former Conservative Cabinet minister, Lord Snowdon and Sam Wanamaker, the film maker.

List of mourners, page 13

Henry still worked when he was more than 80 years old. He died on 31 August 1986. He was 88 years old. There was a special service in Westminster Abbey when he died.

This **sculpture** is the largest **bronze** work that Henry ever made. Henry made it just one year before he died.

Timeline

1898	Henry Moore is born in Castleford, Yorkshire on 30 July.
1910	Henry enters Castleford Grammar School.
1914–18	The **First World War** is fought.
1917	Henry joins the Army and fights in the First World War.
1921	Henry enters the Royal College of Art, London, on a scholarship.
1924	Henry's first **sculptures** are shown in London.
1928	Henry's first one-man **exhibition** in London.
1929	Henry marries Irina Radestsky and completes major work for London Underground.
1938	Henry takes part in the International Exhibition of **Abstract Art** in the Netherlands.
1939–45	The **Second World War** is fought.
1941	Henry is made an Official War Artist.
1940s	Henry has exhibitions in USA, Australia, Belgium, and other countries.
1948	Henry wins International Prize for Sculpture in Venice.
1955	Henry is made a Companion of Honour in Great Britain.
1977	Henry Moore Foundation begins work in Much Haddam, England.
1986	Henry dies in Perry Green, Hertfordshire on 31 August.

Glossary

abstract art art that tries to show ideas rather than the way things look

bronze type of metal

carve cut into a shape

commission being asked to make a piece of art

exhibition public showing of art

First World War the war in Europe that lasted from 1914 to 1918

hollow having an empty inside

miner someone who works underground to dig for coal

roll of honour list of names of people who have fought in a war

sculpture piece of art that has been made out of stone, wood, or other materials

Second World War the war that was fought in Europe, Africa and Asia from 1939 to 1945

sketch another word for a drawing

studio special room or building where an artist works

tender showing kindness and gentleness

More books to read

The Children's Book of Art, Rosie Dickens (Usborne Publishing, 2005)

More sculptures to see

Large Reclining Figure, Henry Moore, The Henry Moore Foundation

Two Piece Reclining Figure: Points, Henry Moore, The Henry Moore Foundation

Mask, Henry Moore, Tate Gallery, London

Index